Were You There?

Drama For
Lent Or Easter

Raymond I. Keffer

CSS Publishing Company, Inc., Lima, Ohio

WERE YOU THERE?

For more information about CSS Publishing Company resources, visit our website at www.csspub.com.

ISBN 0-7880-1789-6
PRINTED IN U.S.A.

Dedicated to "Redeemed Friends":

Jack LaMarca
Owen Phillips
Howard Reynolds
Rex Campbell

and to my beloved wife, Gail

The Cast

The cast may be of all ages and gender for an intergenerational experience just as these days in the life and death of Christ are meant to speak to his glory for people of all ages.

The cast in order of appearance:

Announcer A: Benjamin, a veteran radio announcer who has been in radio a long time and is the news anchor for the radio station.

Announcer B: Joshua, a young radio announcer who is learning his trade by doing odd assignments like this street interview assignment which deals with the death and resurrection of Christ.

Child A, Child B, and Child C: these are children of upper grade elementary students, grades 4, 5, and 6. They should be different heights to represent children of all ages.

Roman Soldier: a person of many campaigns who has seen death, yet is moved by the death of Christ. He is hard in appearance, but is one who believes in justice and fairness. He is unhappy in a foreign land.

Peter: an imposing person, but one who has had the drive and purpose taken out of his life with the arrest and death of Christ. He now fears life and the future.

John: a middle-aged person who is quiet, trustworthy, and dedicated to Jesus in every way. He has been given the honor of caring for Mary, the mother of Jesus.

Mary: a middle-aged lady who knows her Son is the Messiah, and is deeply moved by his death, yet remains strong in her belief he is fulfilling God's will just as she did as a young maiden.

Rabbi: a man of any age who thinks the right thing was done when Jesus was crucified, yet he is haunted with the notion that this terrible act of putting Jesus to death may have been a mistake. What if Jesus is who he claimed to be, and he has fulfilled the scriptures which the Rabbi has studied?

Joseph of Arimathea: a kindly, older man, who, although deeply moved by the crucifixion, courageously comes forward to claim the body of Christ. He fears neither man nor death at this point in his life.

Mary Magdalene: a strong, middle-aged woman whose life Jesus has given peace and meaning. Her faith and strength have brought her to the tomb on Sunday morning.

Stage Setting

Scene 1

	Podium		Podium
		Joshua	

Stage Level _____

        Benjamin
        Radio Studio

Joshua walks the stage to talk to the people who are returning from Calvary on Good Friday. Benjamin runs the studio below stage level to control the broadcast going out to the public.

Scene 2

        Joshua and Benjamin   Podium
        Remote Studio
        near the Tomb

Stage Level _____

Joshua and Benjamin are near the tomb and in a position to see people coming and going from the tomb of Christ.

Were You There?

Scene 1

Announcer A: Welcome back to our studios. It's been a very eventful day here in Jerusalem. Let me recap the highlights of the day so far.

The day began with a Jesus of Nazareth being forced by the Romans to drag a heavy wooden cross through the streets of Jerusalem to a hill called Golgotha. This wooden cross was the very cross upon which the Romans were planning to crucify Jesus.

The cross was too heavy for Jesus to carry, and he stumbled many times. The crowds, which lined the streets, mocked and ridiculed Jesus. He was forced to wear a crown of thorns made by the Romans as a part of his torture.

Some of the crowd tried to help Jesus along the way, but the Roman soldiers forced them back and used force at times to keep the crowd from getting out of control. Several arrests were made.

Once Jesus reached Golgotha, they nailed his hands and his feet to the wooden cross he had carried. His cross was lowered into a hole between two thieves who were also being crucified.

The Roman soldiers made a crude sign saying, "King of the Jews," and nailed the sign on the cross above Jesus' head.

As the day wore on, one thief mocked Jesus, saying that if he were really the Son of God, then he should save himself and them as well. The second thief rebuked him for such mockery, and asked Jesus to remember him when Jesus came into his Kingdom. Jesus was heard to say to the second thief, "Truly, I say unto you, today, you shall be with me in Paradise."

A Roman soldier thrust a spear into the side of Jesus to see if he were dead. Jesus groaned, and said, "Father, into Thy hands I commend my spirit." Suddenly, the earth quaked and darkness covered Jerusalem.

Sadness, disbelief, grief, and horror are words that have been used to describe the events of this day. There's much more to be said and reported on this story.

Many people seem to think this was all just a mere coincidence of events which the followers of this man, Jesus, used to fulfill their own beliefs.

Let's go now to our live broadcast booth and talk to some of the people who witnessed the events which shook the world today.

Announcer B: Thank you, Benjamin. We're here on the streets of Jerusalem hoping to talk to people who witnessed the newsbreaking events of this day. I see some children coming. It's late for them to be out. You children, were you there today when Jesus died?

Child A: Yes, we were there. We saw our friend Jesus murdered today by the Romans for no reason at all. He was a good man, and they murdered him. That's not right.

Child B: That's right. He was innocent of any crime, but they killed him instead of that thief, Barabbas. Jesus loved us. He loved all the children. We were always welcome to go to see him.

Child A: The Romans made Jesus drag a heavy cross through the streets. We tried to get to him with some water, but the Romans wouldn't let us. Jesus was thirsty, and we couldn't help him.

Child B: Yeah. I wanted to give Jesus some oil for his cuts, but I couldn't get past the Roman guards. They cursed at us many times to stay back. Jesus never cursed at us. He was our friend.

Child C: Why did they do this to a kind man like Jesus? He always had time for children, and we children know he did nothing wrong. At one corner, Jesus held out his hand to me. He tried to smile, but his pain was too great. He did say one word though, "Love."

Announcer B: Love? What did he mean by that?

Child A: Jesus loved all the little children. Not only Jewish children, but Gentile children, too.

Child B: Yes, he always had time for us. But we lost our friend today on the cross. We saw him murdered.

Child C: Yes, we all saw him die. What kind of adults are they who could murder a loving man like Jesus? They'll pay for their murdering Jesus someday. You just wait and see.

Roman Soldier: All right now, you children, move on! You're blocking the streets. Move on, you little beggars. Move it, I said!

Announcer B: You, sir, were you there? Were you there today when Jesus was nailed to the cross?

Roman Soldier: Who? Me? (*Uneasily, as if worried about others hearing his response to the question*) You fellows go keep the crowd moving, and I'll be right with you.

Now, you wanted to know if I were there when this Jesus was nailed to the cross?

Announcer B: Yes! Were you there?

Roman Soldier: Who wants to know? Are you a spy for the Jewish religious leaders or something?

Announcer B: No, I am a radio news reporter just trying to get information on what happened today as you saw it happen. Were you there at Golgotha when Jesus was crucified and died on a cross?

Roman Soldier: Yes, I was there. Like my fellow Romans, I had no time for this Jesus, nor his fellow trouble-making Jews. I was there when they nailed him to the cross, and when they hoisted the cross upright into the ground. I heard his pain then, and I can still hear it.

Announcer B: What was it like? Can you describe it for us?

Roman Soldier: It was the pain of an innocent man. Not like the painful cries of the two thieves who died on either side of Jesus. They cried out in pain as other men cried out in pain during these crucifixions, that's normal.

But his cry was different. He was different. He didn't curse and spit on us. He forgave us. He said we were only following orders and doing the will of others. He seemed delirious. He kept talking to his father, and he wanted to know why his father had forsaken him. He was not in his right mind, I tell you. He was not in his right mind.

Announcer B: Was he right? Were you doing the will of others like the Jewish religious leaders?

Roman Soldier: I cannot answer that. Regulations. I can tell you this, however. He was someone special!

Announcer B: What do you mean special?

Roman Soldier: They said he claimed to be the Messiah, and that he came into the world to save us all from our sins. When I thrust my spear into his side to see if he were dead, his blood squirted upon my face.

Announcer B: So...?

Roman Soldier: When I washed his blood off my face, my eye, which has been badly crossed since birth, was normal. The scars on my face were healed. I was whole. How could an ordinary man's blood do that? He had to be the Messiah! I have no doubts now. He was the Messiah. I believe it.

If a thief can be forgiven on the cross and be with Jesus today in Paradise, then a Roman soldier who was healed with his blood will be with Jesus also. Ahhhh, I must be going. I've got to get back to my barracks.

Announcer B: Thank you. Interesting words from a Roman soldier. But he cannot be right about his healing, and who this Jesus really was.

I think the problems of the day and the heat must have gotten to him. A thief and a Roman soldier in Paradise, really now! Let's ask that man. You sir, may I have a minute of your time?

Peter: Who? Me?

Announcer B: Yes, you. Did you hear that man say that this Jesus who died today was the long-awaited Messiah?

Peter: Yes, I did.

Announcer B: Do you believe that this Jesus was the Messiah?

Peter: Yes. I believe that Jesus was the Messiah as foretold in the scriptures. Any Jewish rabbi or scholar should know that, if they read the scriptures with a pure, honest heart.

The life of Jesus fulfills all the scriptures that were written about the Messiah. John the Baptist lead the way as foretold; Jesus preached salvation to the poor, his own people denied him, and he died on a tree as was foretold.

Announcer B: How can you be so sure? Wait a minute. I know you. Aren't you one of his disciples? Ah — Peter? That's right! Peter!

Peter: No, I — I — I'm not a disciple. I — I — I didn't know this Jesus personally. I only know what others say about him. You'll have to ask those questions of someone more knowledgeable than I.

I'm just a poor, uneducated, Jewish fisherman. You must be confusing me with, who did you say, ah, Peter? Yes, Peter.

Announcer B: Strange. I could have sworn I saw you with him in the garden at Gethsemane the night Jesus was arrested.

Weren't you there with your sword and didn't you cut off an ear of a soldier, and didn't Jesus rebuke you for your violence?

Peter: No. I — I — I wasn't there. I don't know the Jesus you are talking about. You hear me? You must be confused. I don't know anything about Gethsemane or a soldier's ear.

I'm just a poor fisherman. That's right — just a poor fisherman who is visiting friends in Jerusalem for the holidays. Just a poor fisherman. Nothing more. Nothing less.

Announcer B: My apologies, sir. I though surely that you were Peter about whom Jesus said that if you followed him he would make you a fisher of men, and that you were the rock upon which he was going to build his church.

Peter: Oh, no! You are mistaken. I fish for real fish. See these hands? These are the hands of a fisherman, not a disciple.

I'm just a poor fisherman. I'm no rock. I'm no disciple. I'm a nobody. Just another Jew. I never saw this Jesus until today, I swear. (*Pauses*) What was that?

Announcer B: What was what?

Peter: I thought I heard a cock crow. Tell me, did you hear a cock crow?

Announcer B: Oh, that. Yes, I heard a cock crow. Why? Is a cock crowing supposed to mean something? Cocks do that every day.

Peter: My God, forgive me. Forgive me. I did forsake him, not once but three times just like he said I would. (*Rushes off stage*) Forgive me! Forgive me!

Announcer B: Wait! Wait! I have some more questions. Ah, he's gone. Strange fellow. I thought surely he was Peter, the disciple. Oh well.

Let's look for more people who witnessed the events of this day. You, sir, were you there today? This seems to have been a very hard time for you. Why are you weeping? Who are those women with you?

John: Are you unaware of what has happened today? Do you not know that an innocent man, Jesus, has been unjustly crucified today?

How can you be so uninformed? Have you no respect for his mother in her sorrow? Shame on you, sir.

Announcer B: My sincere apologies. I'm very sorry, sir. I didn't recognize you. My sympathy to you, ma'am. You're John, aren't you? One of his disciples, and if she's his mother, she must be Mary!

John: Yes, I'm John. I tell you that those who did this today will rot in hell. Jesus was innocent. He was the long-awaited Messiah, but his own people rejected him, just as he said they would.

He came in peace and love, but they rejected his peace and love. They had him murdered today, those lofty religious leaders, but death will not stop him nor his church. He said that he'd be back to claim his saints, and I believe that he will come again, and soon!

Mary: My son did no wrong. He was sinless. He was willing to take the sins of all humankind and die for us, which he did today. He has always done well for others.

He loved his enemies and blessed them. Even today he forgave his murderers. He died today so that we might live! How blind our people are!

Announcer B: What do you mean, he died that we might live?

Mary: Unless you believe that my son, Jesus, was the Son of God and that he died for you to save you from sin, you are destined to spend eternity in Hell with those who murdered him today.

Announcer B: Is that all? Just believe that? That he was the Son of God and that he died for me? That's all? That's too easy.

John: It may be easy for you to die to self and believe, but you need only to look around today at all the people who cannot die to self. They're the ones who murdered him.

Rather than accept Jesus as the promised Messiah, they chose to follow their own selfish desires in order for them to keep their earthly power and positions. Fools that they are.

Announcer B: There's talk that Jesus will rise from the dead in three days. Do you think there is any truth to that rumor?

Mary: If my son said that he would rise from the dead in three days, then he'll do it! My heart is too heavy today to think about that.

My firstborn is dead, and it was all I could do today to stand by helplessly and watch him die. Oh John, my new beloved son, please take me home.

John: Gladly! I promised Jesus that I'd take care of you, and I shall. I'll love and provide for you as I did my own mother.

(*Mary and John exit; Rabbi enters*)

Announcer B: Rabbi! Rabbi! Do you have a second to talk to us?

Rabbi: I must be getting home. Well ... I can give you a few minutes. What do you want?

Announcer B: Were you there when this Jesus died?

Rabbi: Yes, I was there. So?

Announcer B: Rabbi, it has been reported that when Jesus died, there was an earthquake. Any truth to that?

Rabbi: Just a coincidence, that's all, just a coincidence. The astrologers had predicted this many months ago. It was a normal time for the earth to quake and the sun to be blotted out. Just a coincidence, that's all. Nothing more.

16

Announcer B: It is reported that the last words of Jesus were, "Father, forgive them for they know not what they are doing."

Rabbi: Yes, he said that, but he couldn't have meant it as he cried out earlier, "Father, Father, why have you forsaken me?"

Now tell me, if his Father had forsaken him, how can his Father hear him to forgive anyone! Sheer lunacy, I tell you. Lunacy.

Announcer B: But our reports are that he made those statements hours apart.

Rabbi: What's the difference? He said them, that's all that matters. Besides, if he were God's Son, God would never have allowed his Son to die like a common thief.

Our God is all-knowing and all-powerful. His Son would never have died like that. The heavenly army of angels would have come to his rescue. God's Son would never be a sacrificial lamb; he would be a warrior and free us from these Romans.

Announcer B: But isn't it written that the Messiah will die upon a tree as a living sacrifice, and that he will be forsaken by his own people?

Rabbi: You're quoting scriptures for your own use, and I have no more time for such talk. Jesus was a fake. A false prophet who got what everyone gets who utters blasphemous statements about our God, Jehovah.

A Messiah indeed! (*Exits hastily*)

Announcer B: But ... He's gone, and it's getting dark. Time for one last comment. Oh, wait! You sir, what's the hurry?

Joseph: Time is of the essence. I must see to it that Jesus is buried before sundown as is our Jewish custom.

Announcer B: Who are you, and why is the burial so important to you?

Joseph: I am Joseph of Arimathea. I am a follower of Jesus, and I must provide him with a proper Jewish burial. My heart is heavy, and it is the least I can do for him.

Announcer B: That's dangerous talk, a follower of Jesus. You'd better be careful.

Joseph: Careful, indeed! Jesus is the Messiah, and I fear no man. Jesus was who he said he was. I firmly believe that. His message was clear for everyone with an open heart to hear. He said that he was the Way, the Truth, and the Light. No one can get to the Father except through him.

Announcer B: But you're a rich man, why do you care? Why risk your wealth and position for a dead prophet? You have everything to lose.

Joseph: No, I have everything to gain if I accept him as my Savior and everything to lose if I don't accept Jesus. Jesus came to save the rich and poor alike.

He promised that in his house there are many mansions, and that he has room for all of his believers. I believe, therefore, I must make room for his burial as a final act of love for him as he prepares a place for me in Heaven.

Announcer B: But where are you going to find a grave for a proper burial on such short notice?

Joseph: Jesus will be buried in the tomb that I had prepared for myself. It's the least I could do for him after all that he has done for me, a sinner.

Announcer B: One last question: What about the belief that Jesus will rise from the dead in three days?

Joseph: If Jesus said it, then he'll do it. Pray excuse me, I'm going. It's very late.

Announcer B: Well, folks, this radio mike will be at the tomb of Joseph of Arimathea in three days to see if Jesus will rise from the dead as we have heard.

Think about all that has happened and been said today, and we'll try to put it all together for you during our weekend newscasts. Shalom.

Special Music

Scene 2

(Morning of the third day)

Announcer A: Well, Jesus has been dead for three days. Some of his followers say he'll rise from the dead today. We're here at the tomb to see if this promise comes to pass. It's cold out here this morning.

Ah, I see some people in white approaching the tomb. Ladies! Ladies, may I have a word with you? ... I — I — I guess not. One was crying and the others were very somber.

Announcer B: Whoa! (*Pauses*) What was that? Another earthquake. There's a light so bright I cannot see; it's blinding. It'll take a minute for my eyes to recover. There was a noise like falling rocks also. What could this all mean?

Announcer A: Rest a minute, and I'll try to ask this lady what she saw. You ma'am, were you at the tomb?

Mary Magdalene: (*Rejoices*) Yes. Oh, yes I was.

Announcer A: Tell us what happened. What were that bright light and all that noise?

Mary Magdalene: I've been reborn. My heart leaps with joy and happiness. I'm on my way back home to share my good news with the others.

Announcer A: What good news? Weren't you part of a group of ladies I saw crying a little while ago?

Mary Magdalene: Yes, but that was before.

Announcer B: Before what?

Mary Magdalene: That's before I heard him say, "Mary."

Announcer B: Heard whom say, "Mary"?

Mary Magdalene: Why, Jesus, of course. To my great joy, he has risen from the dead as he said he would. I didn't understand when he told us that if they would destroy this temple, he would raise it up in three days, but I do now.

He lives. He has conquered death. When the other ladies and I came here this morning, we were grieving Jesus' death. Our pain was too much. When we got here, an angel was sitting on a rock and said to us that Jesus had risen as he said he would. I was in shock and disbelief. Was this some joke?

I wasn't prepared to find an angel at the tomb. I came to mourn. I saw another white-clothed figure, and I cried out to him, "Please, sir. I beg you, tell me where he has been taken so that I may see to his proper burial."

The stranger asked why I was seeking the living among the dead.

Announcer A: The whom? Tell us more, more.

Mary Magdalene: As I continued to weep, the stranger came closer to me. I did not recognize him through my tears. I said, "Sir, can you tell me where they have taken my master?"

Then in an instant I knew that the man was Jesus. He said, "Mary." No one said my name as sweet as Jesus did. He is alive. He has risen. He has conquered death.

I was overcome with joy. He said not to touch him as yet, but that he would visit the disciples soon, and that I should tell them he is alive.

Tell all of your listeners that Jesus has risen, and that when someone says, "He has risen," they are to respond, "He has risen indeed!" I must go now and share my wonderful news with others.

Announcer B: What more can I say? You just heard Mary Magdalene, an eyewitness who saw Jesus die, who now has seen Jesus alive! If you were there when he was tortured, tormented, and died, you too must be experiencing the joyous news which Mary Magdalene has brought to all of us, Jew and Gentile alike.

Announcer A: What an exciting turn of events! If these things are true, those who thought to silence Jesus and his ministry by having the Romans put him to death have failed.

With the strength of his resurrection from the dead, his disciples and followers have nothing to fear now that death has been conquered. Jesus will be more of a problem to the Jewish religious authorities now than before he died.

Announcer B: Right. The ultimate fear that authorities had, death, has been conquered. The zeal of Joseph of Arimathea and now Mary Magdalene is sure to spread to others now that Jesus is alive.

Announcers A and B: Jesus has risen!

Audience: Jesus has risen indeed!